BUILD A BETTER US

A Better Her

31 DAILY CHALLENGES

FOR WOMEN TO LOVE GOD,
THEMSELVES & OTHERS BETTER

VANJA & BJ THOMPSON

Written by **Vanja & BJ Thompson**

Edited by **Danielle Anderson**

Cover & Interior design by **Melissa Webster**

Interior Format & Layout by **Melissa Webster**

31DAYGROWTHCHALLENGE.COM

And he said to him, "You shall love the Lord your God with all your heart and with all your soul and with all your mind. This is the great and first commandment. And a second is like it: You shall love your neighbor as yourself."

Matthew
22:37-39

Table of Contents

OUR LETTER TO YOU

If we're honest, we can all do better in the areas of faith, relationships, and self-care. Growth in these essential areas won't happen magically; it requires that you and I are proactive and intentional about developing habits that lead to meaningful transformation. We can both personally attest to passively waiting for growth to happen in relationships, personal care, and faith, only to realize we were grossly immature. We had to decide to stop making excuses, create habits, and stick to a regimen that led to a better me, which led to a better us.

A Better Her is a 31-day challenge that lays out simple ways to create significant health in these critical areas. Based on the biblical call to "Love God, Love yourself, and Love others," this resource is meant to give the reader simple yet effective practices that bring life to your faith, relationships, and self-care. It's not a magic formula for growth, but rather a set of daily exercises meant to encourage growth in each area. Like any challenge or training, whatever you put in is what you'll get out. Take these challenges seriously, and you'll see serious results. Take these challenges minimally, and you'll see minimal results. Writing this book was a joint effort, but it is I, Vanja, who is speaking to you in the challenges. The 31-day growth challenge is for all women no matter your status, but if necessary, feel free to modify any challenge so that it better fits your unique situation, time restraints, or context.

NOW, LET'S GET STARTED!!!

Dear Lord,

We pray that you give this woman courage to relinquish control and pursue a level of uncomfortable growth that makes your grace evident. Give her deep joy, increased love, and a re-energized soul. We pray for restored relationships, tangible charity towards others, and self-reflection that leads to life transformation and a new trajectory. We pray for deep and rich experiences that create lasting memories with others, herself, and You.

IN JESUS' NAME, AMEN.

Getting the most out of this book

The challenges in this book are organized under three pillars—**Faith, Others, Self-care**—representing the three distinct areas of intentional growth. It is up to you to determine the order in which you will complete the pillars, but once you've started a pillar, please complete the challenges within that specific pillar in the order prescribed.

For example, you may choose to complete the pillars in this order—Faith, Self-Care, Others. If so, here is what your 31-day journey would look like:

> **FAITH**: DAYS 1-10
> **SELF-CARE**: DAYS 11-21
> **OTHERS**: DAYS 22-31

If you choose to complete the pillars in this order—Self-Care, Others, Faith—here is what your 31-day journey would look like:

> **SELF-CARE**: DAYS 1-11
> **OTHERS**: DAYS 12-21
> **FAITH**: DAYS 22-31

HERE ARE A FEW RULES TO HELP YOU GET THE MOST OUT OF THIS 31-DAY CHALLENGE:

(1) Limit your social media use to 30 minutes a day. In place of social media usage, practice the challenges, be present in your relationships, and be okay with spending time in silence and solitude so that you might get to know yourself.

(2) Daily journal your experiences, feelings, and revelations.

(3) Take this challenge with one other person or designate an accountability partner with whom you can process your experiences.

The goal of this 31-day challenge is to help you become more intentional and present in the areas of life that matter most. If you miss a day (or days), be gracious with yourself and catch up as soon as you are able. Remember, the more consistent you are, the more you'll see the benefits of the challenges.

HERE IS WHAT YOU CAN EXPECT TO SEE IN EACH DAILY CHALLENGE:

- *Cost to You icons* - these help you better grasp the time and financial commitment of the challenge.

$$\boxed{\frac{30}{\text{MIN}}}$$ = 30 MINUTES

$$\boxed{\frac{24}{\text{HRS}}}$$ = CHALLENGE LASTS 24 HOURS

$$\boxed{\frac{10}{\$}}$$ = $10.00

- *Personal story* - a short story from our own lives that will help illustrate the lesson
- *Truth* - a brief statement capturing that day's fundamental idea
- *Challenge* - the prescribed action for that day
- *Reflection* - Emotions, thoughts, & actions experienced?

Following each daily challenge there is designated space for you to journal. Ask yourself key questions and write your responses. What did you feel? What did you experience? What were some new thoughts?

PICK ONE

 x 10

Do your best to present yourself to God as one approved, a worker who has no need to be ashamed, rightly handling the word of truth.
2 Timothy 2:15

Years ago, while two of our three kids were still toddlers, I began an early Monday morning bible study. When I say early, I mean 5:30 in the morning early! It was EARLY! The purpose was for us women to experience the significance of truly knowing the Word for ourselves and growing in the ability to teach others. Even though I started the group, I wasn't the primary teacher - it was a group effort. Each lady was assigned a passage to teach one week in advance. We would decide on a book of the bible to dive into and break down the text into smaller sections each Monday. I distinctly remember studying Philippians and deeply desiring each woman to come to the group with such an immense passion and understanding of the text that she would be able to teach it, even if she was not assigned that morning. We soon changed the format to match my heart. Every week, all 10 of us came prepared to teach, and we would draw a name out of a jar to select the lucky teacher for that day's specific text. Looking back, though it was very challenging, it was exhilarating.

Truth Insight

The extent to which a person is willing to study God's word for themselves is the extent to which that person can develop a personal relationship with their Creator.

Challenge

Today, identify a book of the Bible, with five chapters or less, to study. For the next 2 weeks read and reflect on 1 chapter every day for 30 minutes. The book can be relevant to this season of life or a book you've never read or studied before. Here are some helpful questions to ask yourself as you read:

(1) What is the historical background?

(2) Given the historical background and geography, how would the people of that time understand the words of the author?

(3) What are the timeless truths people of today can learn from this verse, chapter or book?

(4) How does this relate to your personal life?

Reflection

_____

_____

_____

_____

_____

_____

_____

MY HEART, YOUR HEART

30
MIN

> *"Nothing teaches us about the preciousness of the Creator as much as when we learn the emptiness of everything else."*
> *- Charles Haddon Spurgeon*

Growing up in the 80's, we did a lot of playing outside. Technology was a luxury for most kids. Granted, we did have an original Nintendo, but we thoroughly enjoyed being outside the majority of the time. One of our favorite outside games was Hide and Go Seek. The goal of the game was to do everything you could to not be found - to remain unseen. One time I hid so well that I eventually had to come out because everyone stopped looking for me. With today's technology and social networking tools, it's easy for us to seem connected to everyone, in seemingly the most intimate of ways, and yet still feel unseen. You and I were made for deep connection with God and people, but that type of relationship demands we become vulnerable, not just connected.

Truth Insight

Your Father in Heaven knows and sees you, but to fully experience being fully known by Him will demand intentional and consistent vulnerability.

Challenge

Today, carve out 30 minutes to practice vulnerability with God (phone on airplane mode). Incorporate worship music if you can. Feel free to sing loudly, raise your arms, clap, weep, or whatever else you feel compelled to do.

Reflection

_____

_____

_____

_____

_____

_____

_____

_____

_____

_____

_____

_____

_____

_____

_____

GROWING CLOSER

30
MIN

...pray without ceasing...
1 Thessalonians 5:17

Being an extrovert, I continuously find myself engaging the people around me! If it's not hosting a small gathering in our home, it's going to someone else's gathering, counseling and advising others, attending a small group, spending time with my family, and other spur-of-the-moment adventures! But I've found that when I fail to schedule a time to pause and hear from God, and not others, those seemingly pleasant moments become unending and, eventually, overwhelming. The older and wiser I grow, the more I realize that scheduled time with God, apart from others, brings intimacy with Him and joy in my life.

Truth Insight

In Psalms 46 it's clear that God is making Himself available to be known by those who are still and recognize Him for who He is.

Challenge

Today, spend some time with the God who knows you genuinely by taking a 30-minute prayer walk. Try to find a space outside where you can speak freely and without interruption. Talk with God about what you're celebrating, concerned for, or need Him to change. If you're a mom at home with small children, ask for assistance or take the kids for a walk as you pray.

Reflection

_____

_____

_____

_____

_____

_____

_____

_____

_____

_____

_____

_____

———————————————————————

———————————————————————

———————————————————————

———————————————————————

———————————————————————

———————————————————————

———————————————————————

———————————————————————

———————————————————————

———————————————————————

———————————————————————

———————————————————————

———————————————————————

———————————————————————

———————————————————————

———————————————————————

———————————————————————

———————————————————————

———————————————————————

———————————————————————

GENEROSITY

"In all things I have shown you that by working hard in this way we must help the weak and remember the words of the Lord Jesus, how he himself said, 'It is more blessed to give than to receive.'"
Acts 20:35

I consider myself a very giving person, but there are many times that I forget to plan on strategic ways to give intentionally. It's great to give spontaneously to those we see in need, but it's also important that we prioritize giving to organizations that provide holistic support - physical, spiritual, mental, relational, and so on. Our family often prays and talks about places we'd like to give strategically and the reason why. Including our children in the process is a priority, because I think it is a practical step to help fight against entitled mindsets that may develop in them. This practice has helped remind every member of our family that even our earned money and free time belongs, not to us, but to God.

Truth Insight

The more we give to charities and organizations that support human life, the more we fulfill Jesus' command to "love our neighbor as ourselves."

Challenge

Today, choose a public charity or organization whose work you'd like to see expanded in the world, then give a financial gift. If you have a spouse or children, bring them into the conversation. The amount doesn't matter, but it has to be monetary.

Reflection

_____

_____

_____

_____

_____

_____

_____

_____

_____

_____

_____

_____

_____

_____

_____

_____

_____

_____

_____

_____

_____

_____

_____

_____

_____

_____

_____

_____

_____

_____

_____

_____

STICKY NOTES

30	30
MIN	MIN

> "*Remember your connection with the cosmos. Remember your connection with the infinity and that remembrance will give you the freedom.*"
> - Amit Rah

I'm sure I wasn't the only kid told that if you swallow a watermelon seed, a watermelon would soon grow in your stomach. I remember, after accidentally eating a few of those tiny seeds, being afraid that my stomach would grow to an enormous size. At times I couldn't even enjoy a juicy, sweet watermelon without some form of anxiety. As a child, it's easy to be deceived because we are incredibly dependent on those around us for correct information. I remember being told lies by my cousin that ended in not-so-good consequences. If believing a lie about the world can lead to profound confusion and poor experiences, the same is true about God.

Truth Insight
Experiencing God will mean that we learn the truth about Him so that our experiences match His intended purposes.

Challenge

Today, look through your bible for 5 truths you need to remember about God's character. Write them on sticky notes and place them where you can see them easily so that you will regularly be reminded of God's truth.

Reflection

_____

_____

_____

_____

_____

_____

_____

_____

_____

_____

_____

_____

_____

_____

_____

_____

_____

_____

_____

_____

_____

_____

_____

_____

_____

_____

_____

_____

_____

_____

_____

_____

_____

_____

DESPERATE

<table>
<tr><td>24
HRS</td><td>"Fasting is the first principle of medicine; fast and see the strength of the spirit reveal itself."
- Rumi</td></tr>
</table>

The Bible tells the story of a woman who, after suffering from an issue of blood for twelve years, touches Jesus and is instantly healed. Due to her illness, this woman was desperate and found herself pressing through a large crowd just to touch the end of Jesus' garment. Why go through all of that inconvenience? She believed what she was giving up in personal comfort or looking foolish amongst the crowd, couldn't compare to what she could gain. We live in a nation that highly values personal comfort. Everything - from how we eat, to what we drive, to where we live. Everything in my everyday experience says that my pleasure and enjoyment is to be guarded and protected at all cost. Though personal comfort is readily available, connection to my Creator, leading to deep joy, demands I become uncomfortable.

Truth Insight
In the pursuit of joy, you won't intentionally become uncomfortable until you believe that Jesus has something great.

Challenge

Today, make yourself uncomfortable so you can experience deeper joy. Resolve to go at least 24 hours without drinking and eating sugar or whatever you deem as your go-to comfort food or drink. It may not be easy, but it will be worth it. When you feel the pain of no sugars or carbs, pray to remind yourself you want more of God.

Reflection

_____

_____

_____

_____

_____

_____

_____

_____

_____

_____

_____

_____

_____

_____

LIBERATED

30 MIN	30 MIN

"The enemy uses those things you're insecure about. Free yourself and take your power back by being secure in who you are—flaws and all."
- Yvonne Pierre

The rise of social media has been both a blessing and a challenge. It's incredible to have the capacity to connect with friends, family, and classmates without the pressure of maintaining a presentable profile. I can just lay in my bed in a pair of comfy sweats and a t-shirt with messy hair and crust in my eyes. The challenge though is the never-ending array of various images of beauty that come across my timeline. Everything from women in bikinis, to immaculate manicures and perfectly contoured faces, to Beyoncé, after giving birth to twins, looking amazing. No matter how confident we may be about our body or appearance, these images can perpetuate deep insecurities about how God naturally made us. The more I find myself scrolling and liking the pictures of friends and celebrities, the more I find myself asking if I'm actually enough. Our insecurities keep us from contentment because we're always comparing ourselves to others. No matter who you are, God says you are "fearfully and wonderfully made." That means God uniquely made you in your body, and it's beautiful.

Truth Insight

When we agree with God about who we are, we can find contentment, but that means being honest with Him about our insecurities.

Challenge

Today, write out all the areas of your body or your looks where you have insecurity. Once you've identified these areas, take time to look at yourself bare in front of the mirror so that you can relearn yourself as being wonderfully made by God.

Reflection

_____

_____

_____

_____

_____

_____

_____

_____

_____

_____

_____

_____

I HEAR YOU

30	30
MIN	MIN

"Education is the kindling of a flame, not the filling of a vessel."
- Socrates

The older I've gotten, the more obvious it is that it's not wise to assume you're the smartest person you know. Doing so reduces our capacity to grow in new ways. Thinking through my friend group and those I interact with on a regular basis, then surrounding myself with people who think differently, allows me to be challenged on world issues, spirituality, relationships, and basic life skills. One area in particular that I lack common knowledge in is science, so I'm intentionally trying to grow in the craft of asking good questions. It's amazing to speak with my friend who could break down anything from the process of a solar eclipse to how certain foods affect your body. I find myself feeling like a first grader at specific points in our conversations but, for growth purposes, I know that it's an excellent place to be.

Truth Insight
The more we intentionally engage our areas of ignorance, the more we grow to be competent in those areas.

Challenge

What's an area you believe you need to grow in? Today, find a podcast or sermon and intently take notes. What did you learn? What are some immediate applications? What's new? What's inspiring? Is there anything you need to investigate further?

Reflection

_____

_____

_____

_____

_____

_____

_____

_____

_____

_____

_____

_____

_____

_____

_____

REFLECTIVE

30	30
MIN	MIN

> *"The beginning of thought is in disagreement - not only with others but also with ourselves."*
> - Eric Hoffee

As a free-spirited person, there is nothing worse than hearing my supervisor say, "Let's meet for our quarterly evaluation." I still cringe thinking about the many times in the past I've sat across from a supervisor as they evaluated every aspect of my work performance. Whose cruel idea was this? As much as I despise these evaluations with my boss, I've realized that without proper assessment, essential areas of life can go unattended for years at a time. Sadly, it often takes a major crisis for us to see the need to invest in a particular area - this is definitely true of our faith.

Truth Insight

Sober reflection and regular tending to various areas of life allow us to experience the abundant life our Creator intended.

Challenge

Today, think of 2-3 close friends or family members. Ask them to list 3 of your strengths and 3 weaknesses. It can pertain to spirituality, health, relationships, career, or another topic. Commit to taking the constructive criticism, not in a defeating way, but as a helpful tool to help you genuinely reflect on what is true. I've done this a few times and, though it can be very challenging, it is beneficial. Pray before you read them and know that your identity is in God.

Reflection

_____

_____

_____

_____

_____

_____

_____

_____

_____

_____

_____

_____

_____

_____

_____

_____

_____

_____

_____

_____

_____

_____

_____

_____

_____

_____

_____

_____

_____

_____

_____

_____

I'VE LEARNED

30	30
MIN	MIN

...and what you have heard from me in the presence of many witnesses entrust to faithful men, who will be able to teach others also.
2 Timothy 2:2

Have you ever taken a class or course for an entire semester and by the end, couldn't recall a single thing you learned? (Sadly I've done this more times than I'm willing to admit publicly.) Maybe the presentation of the material didn't connect, the information was irrelevant, or you didn't pay out-of-pocket for the course, so you, literally, were not invested in the class. Information only has an impact to the degree that we can recall, observe, and experience its implications in real life. Too often, people of faith go entire seasons of "learning" truth about God, but can't recall significant details. I'm growing in the habit of reteaching what I have learned. It forces me to own the information and think through it from varying perspectives. Teaching someone else what I've been studying in scripture has proven to be a fruitful exercise.

Truth Insight

The degree to which we learn the truths of God is the degree to which divine intelligence and power are at our disposal.

Challenge

Today, contact a friend, mentee, or co-worker and ask permission to schedule a time to reteach what you've been learning in this book study.

Reflection

_____

_____

_____

_____

_____

_____

_____

_____

_____

_____

_____

_____

_____

_____

_____

_____

MEAL PREP

30 MIN	30 MIN	30 MIN	30 MIN

"The secret to getting ahead is getting started. Today is the day for new beginnings."
- Unknown

Wouldn't it be simpler if our lives weren't so busy and the most convenient foods weren't so unhealthy for our bodies? Eating a consistently healthy diet sounds easy but can be extremely difficult. In some seasons I've found myself eating out of convenience but later feeling guilty. Why? Not just because I may have unknowingly added a few pounds, but because I didn't feel good emotionally. I've learned over time that a poor diet not only impacts my physical body, but it also affects my mood— how I feel. I'm aware that eating is a delicate subject to discuss. We all find ourselves on the spectrum between two dangerous extremes—overeating and self-induced starvation. Regardless of where we fall on the spectrum—and let's be honest, that can change from day to day—everyone needs healthy food. It's challenging, but it's not impossible!

I've found that when I prepare my meals in advance, I make much better choices and, subsequently, keep a positive mood. Eating healthy takes time, thought, and planning. There's a helpful quote illustrating this point: "If you fail to plan, plan to fail."

Truth Insight

Eating healthy has positive impacts on our physical and emotional health.

Challenge

Today, create a meal-prep plan for the next 5 days. Prepare and store healthy meals for lunch and dinner. If you're unsure where to start, look up your favorite healthy meal prep online!

Reflection

_____

_____

_____

_____

_____

_____

_____

_____

_____

_____

_____

_____

_____

HYDRATE

 x 5

"In time and with water, everything changes."
Leonardo da Vinci

For a good portion of my life, I didn't drink enough water. I'd settle for juice, tea, coffee, Dr. Pepper—really anything but H20. But over time, I began to introduce water as a primary liquid. I've made it a routine by adding fresh fruit, veggies, and herbs to enhance the flavor. The benefits of drinking water are crazy amazing! An interesting fact is that water comprises over 60% of our body. More than half of what's flowing under our skin is water! Some of the benefits of drinking water range from improved skin, lower blood pressure, higher brain functionality, increased weight loss, and the list goes on and on. But despite water being accessible (and often free) in most places in the world, many people, myself included, miss the benefits of this vital body agent. We miss these benefits simply because we neglect water and, many times, grab a cup of coffee, juice, or wine instead.

Truth Insight

Proper hydration is key to our bodies functioning properly.

Challenge

How's your water intake? Is it a habit or an inconsistent activity? For the next 5 days, if you're not already drinking the recommended daily amount of water for your size, set a reminder to drink more water. Let's get that daily hydration!

Reflection

_____

_____

_____

_____

_____

_____

_____

_____

_____

_____

_____

_____

_____

TAKE CARE

30 MIN	30 MIN	10 $	10 $

"Allow yourself to enjoy each happy moment in your life."
- Steve Maraboli

Serving others is a great thing, but when that service doesn't include my needs, it can be harmful. Because I'm a wife, mother, daughter, friend, employee, and so much more, the opportunities to serve others is a bottomless pit. I've had plenty of days where I've given all my energy to serve the needs of everyone—everyone except myself. Initially, I viewed days like that as merely my "duty," until I began to feel exhausted, burned out and grumpy towards the people I love! I decided it was time to make some changes. Slowly, my service started to look different. Serving meant creating a reasonable budget, planning regular times on the family calendar for self-care, and saying NO to any request that would interrupt my recharge. Protecting that time was essential. When I initially brought this up to my spouse, he agreed and was more than willing to rearrange the budget so I could have extra money to care for myself.

Truth Insight

It's not selfish to prioritize self-care needs; it increases our capacity to love and serve others.

Challenge

How's your self-care? Do you have a budget, regular time block, and the courage to say NO to outside requests during that time? Today, schedule a time to get either a spa treatment, manicure, pedicure, or your hair done. If you're in a relationship or have children, discuss with them a plan to prioritize your regular self-care. Also, consider planning a childcare swap with other parents so that you may avoid paying extra for a babysitter.

Reflection

_____

_____

_____

_____

_____

_____

_____

_____

_____

_____

_____

_____

_____

_____

_____

_____

_____

_____

_____

_____

_____

_____

_____

_____

_____

_____

_____

_____

_____

_____

_____

_____

SILENCE

30	30
MIN	MIN

"Silence is a source of great strength."
- Lao Tzu

My house can be extremely noisy. We have three children who take after my side of the family, meaning they are very animated and find freedom in loudly expressing themselves. Everyday noises come from wrestling matches or them arguing over whose turn it is to use certain electronics. I know it's bad when, after I've settled in my mind that yelling at them isn't very practical, I begin to embrace their noise as background music. Sometimes I listen to see how it's going to get resolved amongst themselves and score my parenting based on the results. It sounds pathetic, but it can be entertaining. Though noise may be our norm, silence is a necessity. Silence—a time of not speaking, not thinking, not worrying about what's next.

Truth Insight

Silence energizes our soul and reminds us that God is in control, so we don't have to be.

Challenge

Today, practice a time of silence. Draw a bath and sit silently for 30 minutes to an hour. Go all out and add a face mask, bubbles, your favorite beverage, essential oils, or candles. If you're doing this challenge with your spouse, let them know you've been challenged to do a silent reflection bath.

Reflection

_____

_____

_____

_____

_____

_____

_____

_____

_____

_____

_____

_____

_____

_____

CLUTTER

30	30	30
MIN	MIN	MIN

"For every minute spent organizing, an hour is earned."
- Benjamin Franklin

When I met my husband, we were 19 and just a year or two into college. From the first time I visited his dorm room, I realized that he was not the most organized person. The more we got to know each other the more apparent it became to him that I was annoyed by his clutter. It may have looked messy to me and others, but he somehow managed to create a system out of that mess. Worn folders were for classwork, pencils were for math, and crumbled papers were either scratch paper, test reviews, projects, or homework. His clutter started off as tidiness, but over time, things kept piling and piling and, the more he noticed, the more he'd put off cleaning it for later. The first time I helped to organize his room, he admitted that he was hit with a cool breeze of confidence and clarity. Why? I imagine it is because organizing clutter allows us to breathe better, effectively navigate our space, and maximize our comfort.

Truth Insight
Clutter can overwhelm our senses and make us feel stressed; clearing clutter lessens our stress.

Challenge

Today, clean, declutter, or organize something that you've noticed needs some attention, but that you've kept putting off.

Reflection

_____

_____

_____

_____

_____

_____

_____

_____

_____

_____

_____

_____

_____

_____

_____

_____

_____

WALK IT OUT

30	30
MIN	MIN

"Now shall I walk or shall I ride?
'Ride,' Pleasure said;
'Walk,' Joy replied."
- W.H. Davies

More and more our world is becoming addicted to staring at screens. Don't get me wrong, the advancement of technology is mind-blowing, but it also has its downsides—namely our disconnect from nature. I find that there's nothing quite like walking outside, feeling the wind breeze over my body and having sun-kissed skin as I observe the natural elements—preferably at the beach! Stopping to look up in the sky and reflect on scriptures like 1 Corinthians 15:41 is life-giving and refreshing. Many times, I'll observe people walking in nature, be it a trail or at the park, but their technology will so absorb them, they miss the therapeutic benefits and beauty of God's creation.

Truth Insight

Connecting to nature and our community, without distraction, reminds us that being fully present is transformative for our souls.

Challenge

Today, take a walk outside, maybe at a park, within your community, or around a lake. Whatever you do, be fully present and experience the benefits of connecting deeply to God by being very present in His creation. Don't forget to turn your phone on airplane mode.

Reflection

_____

_____

_____

_____

_____

_____

_____

_____

_____

_____

_____

_____

_____

_____

_____

_____

_____

_____

_____

_____

_____

_____

_____

_____

_____

_____

_____

_____

_____

_____

_____

_____

_____

_____

MEDITATE

30	30	30
MIN	MIN	MIN

"Meditation practice isn't about trying to throw ourselves away and become something better; it's about befriending who we are."
- Ani Pema Chodron

Recently we bought a house in the beautiful, but busy, city of Atlanta. I love our neighborhood because these amazingly tall trees surround each house. My favorite space of our home is the screened-in patio that overlooks at least 50 different trees. Having this space triggers a desire for meditation. Meditation is one of the most effective ways to gain inner peace. Most don't take the time to acknowledge and process our emotions. Each day we merely go through the motions: try to meet deadlines, maintain schedules and relationships, care for children, and the list goes on. We train ourselves to manage daily with stress and anxiety. The crazier life gets, the more I realize my need for meditation. I need times of silence and solitude so that I can reflect on the craziness around me and how it is affecting me.

Truth Insight

We can't genuinely care for others if we don't properly care for ourselves.

Challenge

Today, take some time in the middle of the day to do some breathing exercises and acknowledge how you are feeling. Your mind may be tempted to drift towards the past or the future, if so, gently pull your thoughts back to the present. What are you feeling? Whatever it is, accept it. Accept yourself as you are, without judgment. Do this for 2-5 minutes twice today. Journal what you learned. Yoga is also a great way to engage in meditation.

Reflection

_____

_____

_____

_____

_____

_____

_____

_____

_____

_____

_____

_____

_____

_____

_____

_____

_____

_____

_____

_____

_____

_____

_____

_____

_____

_____

_____

_____

_____

_____

_____

_____

EVALUATE

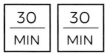

"Attack the evil that is within yourself, rather than attacking the evil that is in others."
- *Confucius*

My middle school years took place during the early 90's when bangs and gel were musts for creating the perfect hairstyle. I was in middle school when my mom allowed me to care for my hair on a daily basis. So I did what any other typical 12-year-old would do - to make sure my hair was flawless, I would use the hot curling iron and as much gel as I could hold in the palm of my hand. Well, it appeared to me months later that high heat from curling irons and chemicals to stiffen your hair is a recipe for breakage. It got to the point that, even if I did want to wear bangs, because of the damage, they looked more like eyelashes. I was distraught and embarrassed. Of course, my mom had to take back that responsibility and resolve the disaster I created. In similar ways, many of us don't give our self-care much thought until our life begins to fall apart. My mom shared with me that I would never have to worry about damaged hair if I just followed a few hair-care tips and paid close attention to how I managed it.

Truth Insight

The difference between people who survive and those who thrive is proactive care, not reactive response.

Challenge

Today, write out, to the best of your ability, what you do for self-care. Would you describe your current state as thriving or surviving? What changes does your routine need? What outside assistance do you need?

Reflection

_____

_____

_____

_____

_____

_____

_____

_____

_____

_____

_____

_____

BOOK IT

30	30
MIN	MIN

"Reading is to the mind what exercise is to the body."
- Joseph Addison

Leisurely reading can be transformative and liberating. I am not a huge book reader and deeply admire my close friend who could spend an entire day in Barnes and Noble. When I do read, though I have a never-ending to-do list with issues continually swirling in my mind, I find that reading for pleasure allows me to escape long enough to catch my breath. I enjoy various types of books—fiction stirs my imagination, memoirs enable me to observe another's life, and non-fiction gives me insight into new things. The times I come across a good read I find myself escaping into another world.

Truth Insight
Leisurely reading can improve overall mental health and expand our understanding of the world.

Challenge
Today, turn your phone on airplane mode, find a peaceful spot, and spend 30 minutes to an hour with a book or article you enjoy.

Reflection

_____

_____

_____

_____

_____

_____

_____

_____

_____

_____

_____

_____

_____

_____

_____

_____

_____

_____

_____

_____

_____

_____

_____

_____

_____

_____

_____

_____

_____

_____

_____

_____

_____

_____

_____

_____

_____

_____

_____

_____

DATE NIGHT

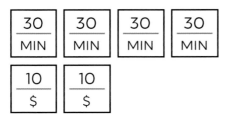

"Life is either a daring adventure or nothing at all."
- Helen Keller

I love the look on my kids' faces when I get dressed up for a date with BJ or ladies' night with my girlfriends. Of course, the first things that come out of their mouths are, "Wow mom! You look pretty!" There are times when BJ and other women will compliment my look, and it's a confidence booster. I am a sucker for comfort. Wearing workout pants and a tank top while lounging on the couch watching Netflix is a norm. So when I receive compliments on my way to a special occasion, it's reassuring and makes me feel pretty. In those moments, I remember the importance of taking pride in my appearance, doing something that gives me energy, and taking time out to have fun. Many of us need to, literally, take ourselves on a date!

Truth Insight

You are a fearfully and wonderfully made image bearer of God. Taking time out to adorn ourselves and celebrate life is a confidence booster and can be great for our souls!

Challenge

Today, plan a self-care date night. Feel free to go alone or invite a friend, family member, or your mate. Shave, style your hair, put on makeup and perfume, and dress in something cute. Eat your favorite meal. Do an activity that energizes you. Eat your favorite sweet. Turn your phone on airplane mode. Take a picture and, if you're on social media, post it with the hashtags #Datenight #31daygrowthchallenge.

Reflection

_____

_____

_____

_____

_____

_____

_____

_____

_____

_____

_____

_____

_____

_____

_____

_____

_____

_____

_____

_____

_____

_____

_____

_____

_____

_____

_____

_____

_____

_____

_____

_____

_____

I FORGIVE

30	30
MIN	MIN

Be kind to one another, tender-hearted, forgiving one another, as God in Christ forgave you.
Ephesians 4:32

My mom raised four children as a single parent, and she never negatively spoke of my father. My father was around, but many visits were few and far between. Whenever he did come around it was always magical and fun. I was a daddy's girl. By my teenage years, I began to see our relationship for what it was—inconsistent. I grew in bitterness to the point of significant resentment. As a young college student, I lived my life as if I didn't need him. I resolved that he would suffer more than me. That mindset began to create discomfort when it was time for me to get married and determine who would walk me down the aisle. I felt too guilty to cheat him of that experience. On my wedding day, there was an unexplainable transformation that took place in my heart towards him as we walked the aisle together. From that day forward, we began to work on our relationship, which led to many honest conversations. He passed away six years later, and I rejoice that we were able to reconcile and enjoy six more years of life together.

Truth Insight

Holding a grudge is more consuming of our energy and time
than it is to forgive; forgiveness is a freeing experience.

Challenge

This one may be the hardest thing you've ever done, but it'll free
you to love with more depth. Today, write a letter to someone you
need to forgive and share the reasons you'd like to forgive them.
This person could be a parent, family member, sibling, mate, or
even yourself.

Reflection

_____

_____

_____

_____

_____

_____

_____

_____

_____

_____

_____

_____

_____

_____

_____

_____

_____

_____

_____

_____

_____

_____

_____

_____

_____

_____

_____

_____

_____

_____

_____

_____

_____

_____

_____

_____

_____

_____

_____

_____

_____

_____

_____

_____

_____

_____

_____

_____

_____

_____

_____

_____

Others

AFFIRMATION

30	30
MIN	MIN

"Affirmations are our mental vitamins, providing the supplementary positive thoughts we need to balance the barrage of negative events and thoughts we experience daily."
- Tia Walker

As a child, I was required to take many medications because of a rare illness I suffered from called vasculitis. One of the drugs I had to take was a steroid called prednisone. Though the steroids helped overcome my primary symptoms, the side effects were devastating to my body and confidence. The medication caused my face to swell—a condition called "moon face." As time went on, I developed a deep sense of insecurity due to the effects of the medication and how others seemed to react to me. It wasn't until high school that my symptoms dissipated, I no longer needed the steroid, and my face and body returned to normal. After I stopped taking the medication, it took years to confront all the insecurities that had built up inside. How would I begin to rebuild my confidence? I didn't exactly know. But the people who knew and loved me started pointing out beautiful things in me that I couldn't see. Slowly, I began to regain my confidence; it continues to be an ongoing journey.

Truth Insight

External affirmation helps us to see things about ourselves that we usually overlook.

Challenge

Today, write down the names of 1-2 friends or family members you want to affirm. What do you see in them that they may not see in themselves? Write them a short letter or email describing the positive things you see.

Reflection

_____

_____

_____

_____

_____

_____

_____

_____

_____

_____

_____

_____

_____

_____

FRIEND CHART

30		30
MIN		MIN

"Courage doesn't happen when you have all the answers. It happens when you are ready to face the questions you have been avoiding your whole life."
- Shannon L. Alder

It's challenging to keep groceries at our house. It seems like days after I've gone shopping my kids start complaining that there's no food. Wait. I *just* went shopping. How is it that there's no food? And sure enough, I open the freezer, fridge, and pantry to see nothing but emptiness. You know it's bad when even the sauces and seasonings are all gone. Before I head to the store again, I take inventory. I make a list of what we have and what we need to function well. This allows me to purchase just enough for our household to enjoy quality meals and be healthy. Sadly, when it comes to relationships, many of us haven't taken inventory in years or potentially ever. Because my husband specializes in human relations, I've been forced to look at my own and make adjustments that would increase my health.

Truth Insight

Taking inventory of friendships helps us identify areas of neglect or overinvestment.

Challenge

Today, take some time and make a list of the friends you have in this season. Why are you friends? What's the purpose? Who do you need to connect with more? Why? Who do you need to add to that list? Who no longer needs to be on the list? Look over this note and attempt to build some weekly routines that help you connect consistently.

Reflection

_____

_____

_____

_____

_____

_____

_____

_____

_____

_____

_____

_____

_____

_____

GIFTS

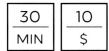

30	10
MIN	$

"It's not how much we give but how much love we put into giving."
- *Mother Teresa*

BJ and I do our best to celebrate major holidays with gifts. Christmas, birthdays, our wedding anniversary, and Mother's and Father's Day are the big ones for us. It's great because on those days I can expect a fun gift from him that I know he invested in—either through significant thought or significant funds. But occasionally on non-holidays, BJ will randomly buy my favorite snack, flowers, or some other small gift just because he was thinking of me. Giving gifts is a sure way to show me love. These sorts of gifts, though inexpensive and not tied to a major holiday, mean so much more to me. I've realized it's not the large celebrations that cause people to feel loved; it's the small thoughtful gifts that remind our friends and family that they're significant to us.

Truth Insight
Small gifts can make significant impacts.

Challenge

Today, buy your mate, family member, or friend a thoughtful gift under $5. What's their favorite snack or ice cream flavor? When they ask why, respond, "No reason, was just thinking of you."

Reflection

_____

_____

_____

_____

_____

_____

_____

_____

_____

_____

_____

_____

_____

_____

_____

_____

THANKFULNESS

30	30
MIN	MIN

"We would worry less if we praised more. Thanksgiving is the enemy of discontent and dissatisfaction."
- H.A. Ironside

Nothing stirs my heart more than a thoughtful note of encouragement. Personal letters are not only instruments to awaken the affections of the recipient, but they also allow the writer to express themselves without ambiguity. Letters can be a powerful tool used to communicate to those who have impacted our lives positively. Many times the recipient is not aware of the scope of their impact, and that could be because we haven't paused long enough to express it with thoughtfulness and clarity. I tried this with my mother once. I had always assumed she knew how much she had positively impacted my life, but when I made it a practice to communicate how much she means to me, she always showed much gratitude. Even though it's a more regular practice now, she is still surprised and caught off guard when I share my appreciation for her. My mom knows my love for her is a constant, but she only came to know her impact by my expressing it.

Truth Insight

Expressing the impact of others in writing gives them a clear sense of how they've positively affected us.

Challenge

Today, write down a list of 10 people you're grateful are a part of your life. Send them a text, private message, or email explaining why you're thankful for them.

Reflection

_____

_____

_____

_____

_____

_____

_____

_____

_____

_____

_____

_____

_____

THE LITTLE THINGS

30	30	30	30
MIN	MIN	MIN	MIN

As each has received a gift, use it to serve one another, as good stewards of God's varied grace.
1 Peter 4:10

My life is busy. Between taking care of our kids, tasks around the house, making time for friends, work, and trying to care for my husband, I find myself regularly stretched to capacity. It's sad to admit, but I'm usually not very good at communicating when I've reached my limit. Thankfully, after sixteen plus years of marriage, my husband has grown to know when I'm beginning to become overwhelmed. He'll say, "Babe, you go rest. I'll cook tonight/clean/take care of the kids." It seems small, but his recognition of my needs energizes me to persevere. It's just the little encouragement I need to keep going. I've realized that voluntarily helping those we care about with small tasks can be just enough motivation for them not to give up.

Truth Insight
Unprompted help with the small tasks can give us a second wind.

Challenge

What's a small task you can assist a family member or friend with? Think about something they have been overwhelmed with and plan a way to serve them. Today, call or message them and ask if you can help them with that task.

Reflection

_____

_____

_____

_____

_____

_____

_____

_____

_____

_____

_____

_____

_____

_____

_____

_____

MOVIE NIGHT

30
MIN

"To get the full value of joy, you must have someone to divide it with."
- Mark Twain

My husband and I couldn't be more opposite in personality. The first time we discovered just how deep our differences ran was when we sat down to pick a movie to see—and this was after we got married. Before marriage I guess we were too infatuated to realize we differed so much on our movie genres of preference. One night we spent over thirty minutes scrolling through Netflix for movies and television shows, and we couldn't find one title we both enjoyed. In the end, we were both so frustrated that we turned off the television and fell asleep. I've since realized that the reason neither of us could agree on a title was because we valued our personal preferences more than we appreciated learning to enjoy the favorites of the other.

Truth Insight

When we lay down our preferences and begin to value those of another, we practice loving them well.

Challenge

Today, ask a friend or family member to let you join them in watching a movie or show they prefer. Watch them light up!

Reflection

_____

_____

_____

_____

_____

_____

_____

_____

_____

_____

_____

_____

_____

_____

_____

_____

TARGET

30	30	10
MIN	MIN	$

> *"The odds of going to the store for a loaf of bread and coming out with only a loaf of bread are three billion to one."*
> *- Erma Bombeck*

I love shopping at Target, or as my friends and I call it, "Tar Zhay." Am I the only person who goes to Target with only one item on my list and ends up with a basket of stuff I saw in the clearance section? Years ago a friend and I would hang out every Tuesday evening finding ourselves at Target, renaming Tuesdays as "Target Tuesday." It's something about the big red circle, the clean aisles, and the smell of Starbucks that gives me extra energy to browse around. My husband is no longer astounded by the sight of me walking through the doors with a few white and red bags in my hand bragging about all my clearance finds. What's better than going to Target and browsing? My friends and I enjoy Target Tuesday and browsing together.

Truth Insight

Inviting others into our life through everyday shared experiences, allows us to create meaningful growth and memorable moments.

Challenge

Today, plan a trip to Target or your favorite retail shop with a friend or family member. What's one item they need? Travel together and enjoy your time browsing the store, even if you don't spend any money.

Reflection

_____

_____

_____

_____

_____

_____

_____

_____

_____

_____

_____

_____

_____

_____

_____

_____

HEARD

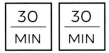

Hear my prayer, O LORD, and give ear to my cry; hold not your peace at my tears! For I am a sojourner with you, a guest, like all my fathers.
Psalm 39:12

It's easy to go through the day interacting with others and not feel remotely connected to any of them—especially on social media. We upload perfect profile pictures and respond to all the questions of "How are you?" with the obligatory "I'm good." All the while we're not. I distinctly remember being 28 and realizing that, even though externally everything seemed okay, internally I was not. I felt utterly alone, unheard, and disconnected, even though I lived a life that was full of people. I lived behind a mask of high energy and smiles, never giving any hints of my internal distress. It wasn't until I conjured up the courage to share what I was feeling with my best friend that I suddenly felt seen, heard, and connected. The experience was not only therapeutic for me, but it also gave my friend and a few others the opportunity to share and plan intentional annual trips where we are honest and vulnerable with our joys, fears, pains, and victories.

Truth Insight

The more we refuse to voice our needs or concerns, the more alone we will feel and the more we will move away from experiencing authentic connection.

Challenge

What are some things you need, concerns you need to voice, or things you need to celebrate? Today, write them on a sheet a paper and share them with a close friend or family member.

Reflection

_____

_____

_____

_____

_____

_____

_____

_____

_____

_____

_____

_____

_____

SORRY

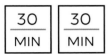

*"Never ruin an apology
with an excuse."*
- Benjamin Franklin

I don't like conflict, especially with those whom I care about
and love. The feeling of anger, the tension throughout my body,
the mental replay of the incident, and the relational strain truly
make me nauseous. I remember one day BJ and I got into a
passionate argument about faults we saw in each other, and I left
frustrated and defeated from his behavior. The more he tried
to point out my wrong, the more I countered with the mistake
of his approach. I finally snapped! I screamed to the point of
pain and stormed out of the suite...we were on a cruise. I was
infuriated. Later, as I reflected on the argument, I realized that,
though he had evident wrongs he needed to own, I'd overreacted
and escalated the conversation. When we spoke again, I wanted
to bring a detailed list of his faults, but instead, I opened the
discussion by apologizing for storming out and screaming. My
sincere apology diffused the anger and allowed us to have an
actual conversation about our disagreement. He hadn't even
considered my storming out as offensive, but I knew it was
something I needed to get off my conscience. My apology showed
vulnerability and humility, which helped to break down his wall
of defensiveness and build a bridge of trust.

Truth Insight

When we apologize for offenses the other person may not even be aware of, relationships can flourish.

Challenge

Today, think of something you've yet to apologize for - in the present or the past. Even if there's nothing obviously wrong, talk with the person and ask for forgiveness.

Reflection

_____

_____

_____

_____

_____

_____

_____

_____

_____

_____

_____

_____

_____

ENTERTAINING ANGELS

Do not neglect to show hospitality to strangers, for thereby some have entertained angels unawares.
Hebrews 13:2

Watching and reading the daily news can be super depressing. I get information about current events from the local news and my social media feed, and they remind me that there is no shortage of negative events and problems in the world. I wouldn't consider myself a pessimist, but with so many issues I can see how many people develop a "glass half empty" mentality. But if we allow our minds to only look at the problems, we'll miss the acts of kindness and goodness happening in our world. Having an eye for goodness enables our hope to be fueled continuously, despite seeing many challenges. One of the ways I rekindle my hopefulness is by doing smalls acts of kindness for strangers. It not only reminds me that life is bigger than me it, hopefully, reminds the recipients that there are still people in the world who selflessly consider and care for others.

Truth Insight

Kindness towards strangers, with no strings attached, imprints a powerful sense of generosity that they will often imitate with others.

Challenge

Today, give a gift to a stranger. Pay for their coffee, meal, gas or choose another activity you feel compelled to do. If at all possible, do it anonymously. But if they ask why, respond, "We need more kindness with no strings attached in this world."

Reflection

_____

_____

_____

_____

_____

_____

_____

_____

_____

_____

_____

_____

_____